A Sample of What's Inside

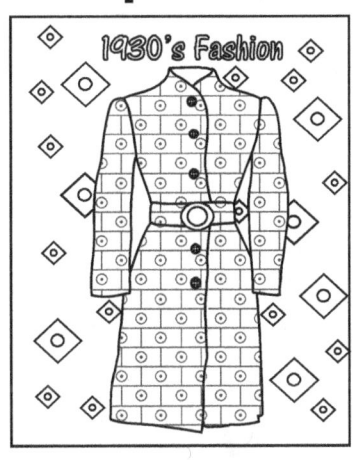

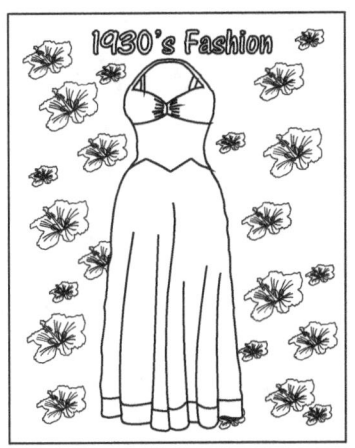

1930'S Vintage Dresses
ADULT COLORING BOOKS
By Beth Ingrias

Want to color
more for FREE?

Get a FREE 25 page adult coloring book
visit
www.BethIngrias.com

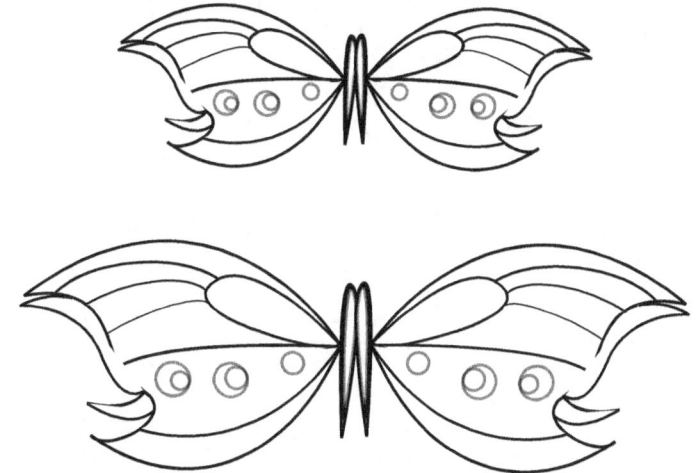

ISBN-13: 978-1533583161
ISBN-10: 1533583161

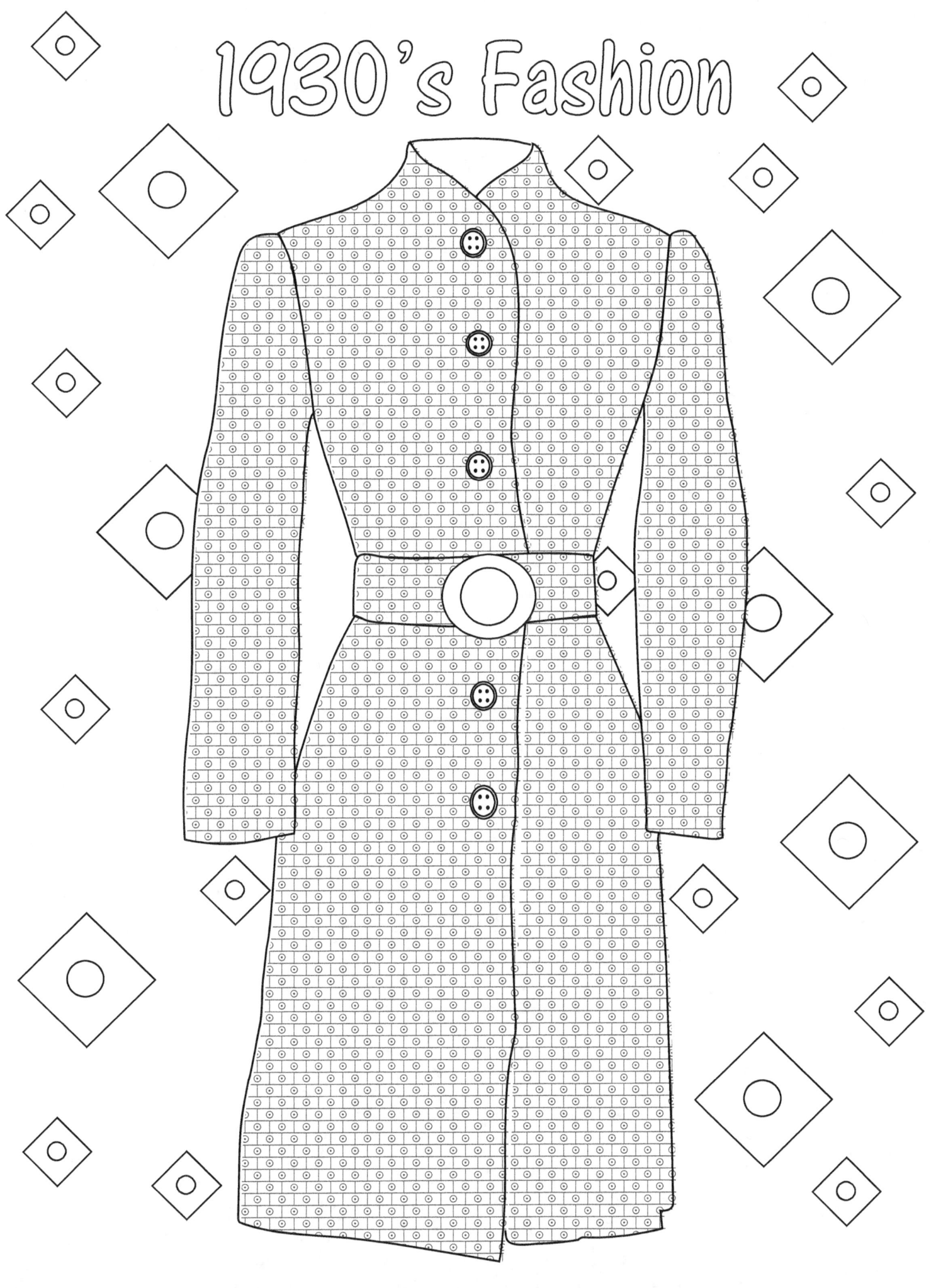

1930's Fashion

1930's Fashion

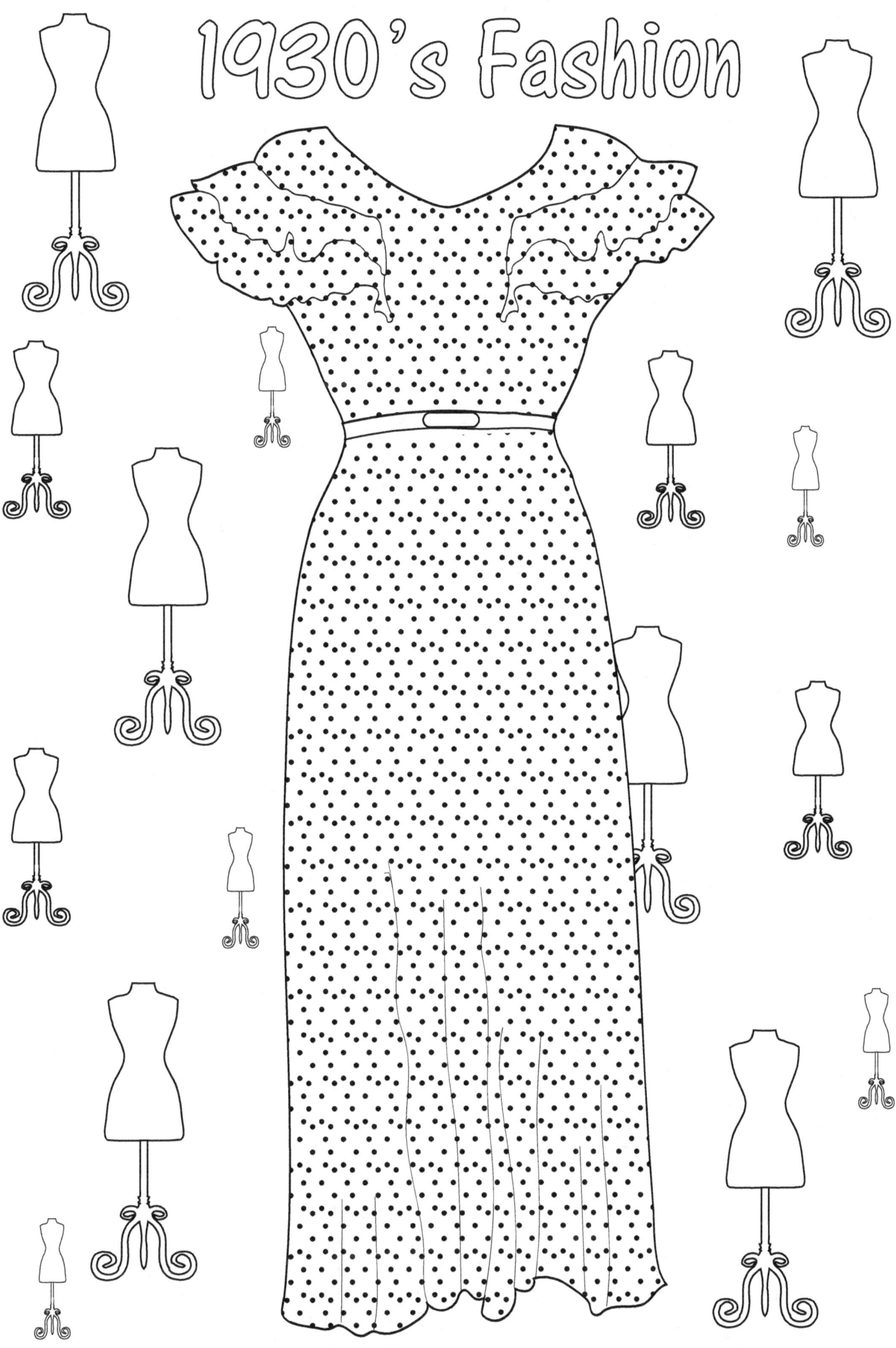

1930's Fashion

1930's Fashion

1930's Fashion

1930's Fashion

1930's Fashion

1930's Fashion

1930's Fashion

1930's Fashion

1930's Fashion

1930's Fashion

1930's Fashion

1930's Fashion

1930's Fashion

1930's Fashion

1930's Fashion

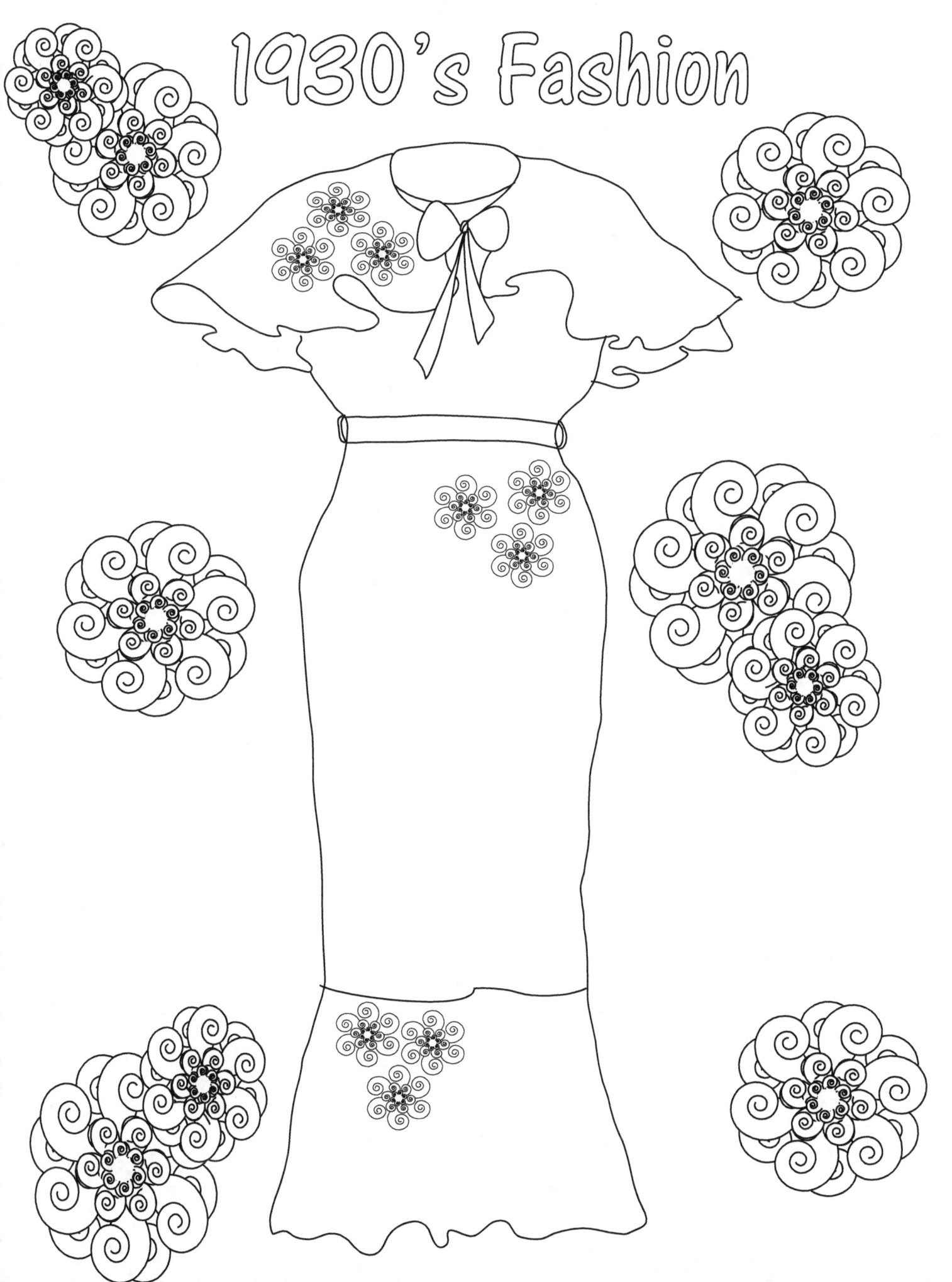

1930's Fashion

1930's Fashion

1930's Fashion

1930's Fashion

1930's Fashion

1930's Fashion

Thanks for picking up a copy of my book. I really appreciate it. If you enjoyed coloring these pages please feel free to leave a review! I would love to hear what you think of my designs.

I would also love to see how you have chosen to color some of my designs. Feel free to email me some pictures of the pages you have colored. You can email me here:

bethingrias@gmail.com

Thanks,
Beth

P.S.
Don't forget to get your free 25 page coloring book at my website.

www.bethingrias.com